LET'S DRAW FUN ANIMALS

In 7 simple Steps!

By Maddie Frost & _____

(Your name here!)

HARPER

An Imprint of HarperCollinsPublishers

This book is dedicated to you. Yes, YOU—YOU!
The YOU about to draw in it right now.

And to my editor and friend, Tamar.

Aww.

Hi!

A NOTE FROM Maddie

Hello, dear artist pals! Get ready to go on a **WILD** and **CRAZY** drawing journey of **EPIC PROPORTIONS**. Just kidding. Well, it might be a little wild, we're drawing **FUN** animals. **ROAR**!

I made this book to make drawing fun. Drawing is hard and frustrating sometimes. Trust me, I know. I've crumpled up LOTS of sketchbook pages. But it doesn't have to be so difficult. So that is why I'm sharing my love for drawing in simple and easy ways. By breaking these critters down into seven shape-based steps, we will end up with successful and satisfying outcomes. Plus you get cool animal facts along the way because animals are the best. It's going to be fun! Now go grab something to draw with and **LET'S DRAW!**

TABLE OF CONTENTS

FARMY FARM → Page 6

RAIN FOREST VIBES → Page 10

YAY PETS → Page 14

ON SAFARI IN THE SAVANNA → Page 20

IN THE WOODS → Page 26

OCEAN DIVE → Page 32

super cute Babies → Page 36

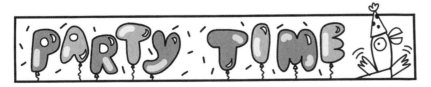
PARTY TIME → Page 40

DIRECTIONS

Follow each of the seven steps to draw
the animal in the empty square.

If you want more space, no worries, just grab a blank piece of paper.

Using a **pencil** or **pen** will work best!

Yay! I erase!

Well, I'm a daredevil!

There are **fun facts** and **drawing tips** throughout the book.
Cool, right? Just keep your eyeballs open for these symbols.

FUN FACT ★

DRAWING TIP

AND DON'T FORGET TO HAVE FUN!

PRACTICE MAKES

~~PERFECT~~
~~PERFF~~
PERFECT

Drawing fun animals takes practice
so let's try a couple to warm up.

Start with **Peep**. You'll see her throughout the book.
She likes to shout.

Now try **Sketch**. You'll see him too.
He's funny (for a cat).

Great job! You're a natural.

LET'S DRAW!

A natural what?

FARMY FARM

Ducky Duck

Moo Cow

HA!

Laughing Rooster

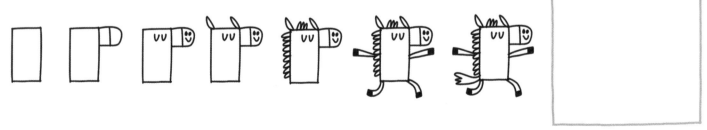

Prancing Horse

FUN FACT

Cows can nap standing up!

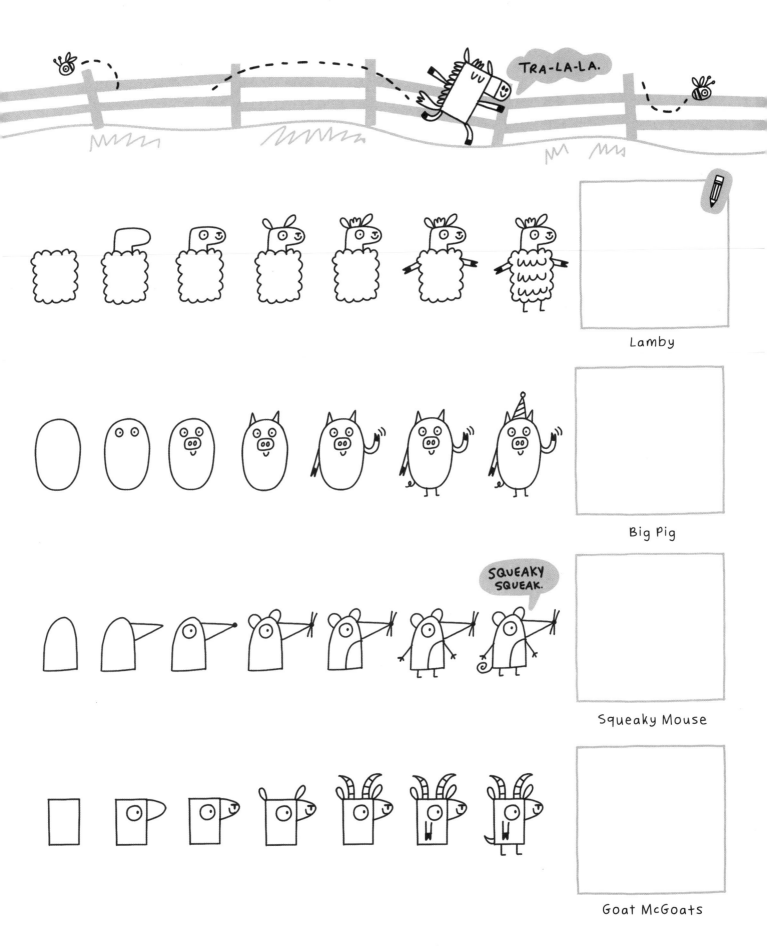

Lamby

Big Pig

SQUEAKY SQUEAK.

Squeaky Mouse

Goat McGoats

DRAWING TIP

The letter "T" is a perfect nose for lambs, llamas, and goats.

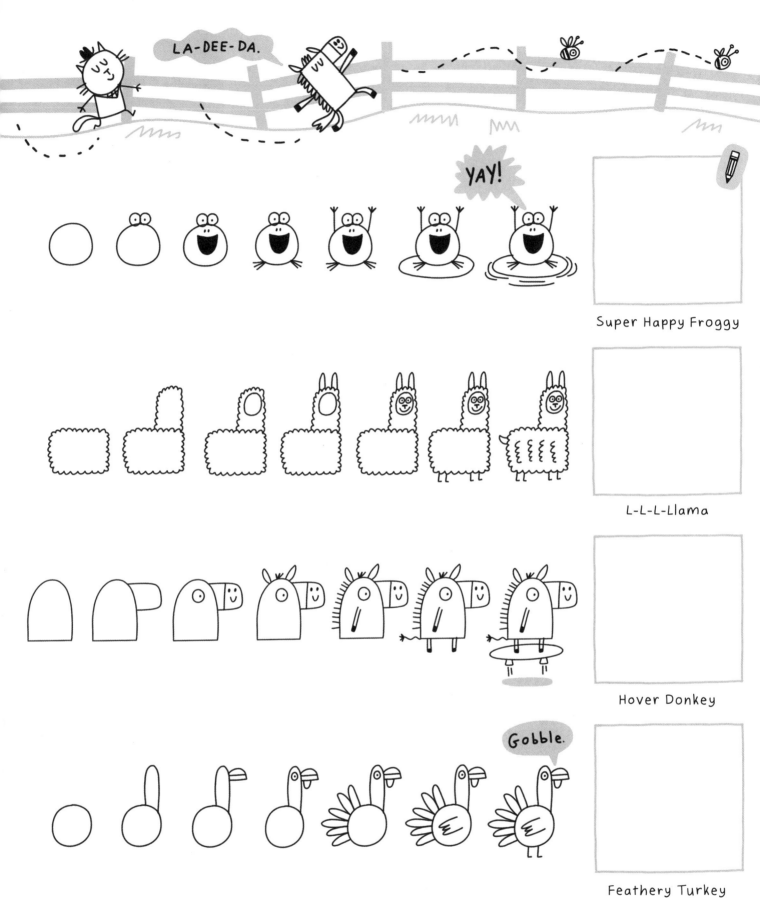

Super Happy Froggy

L-L-L-Llama

Hover Donkey

Feathery Turkey

DRAWING TIP

Playing with the shape of speech bubbles can be really fun.
Try a spiky shape to show an animal shouting.

FARMY FUNTIVITY

What are these friends saying to each other?
Write their dialogue in the word balloons.

Now create your own farmy comic!

RAIN FOREST VIBES

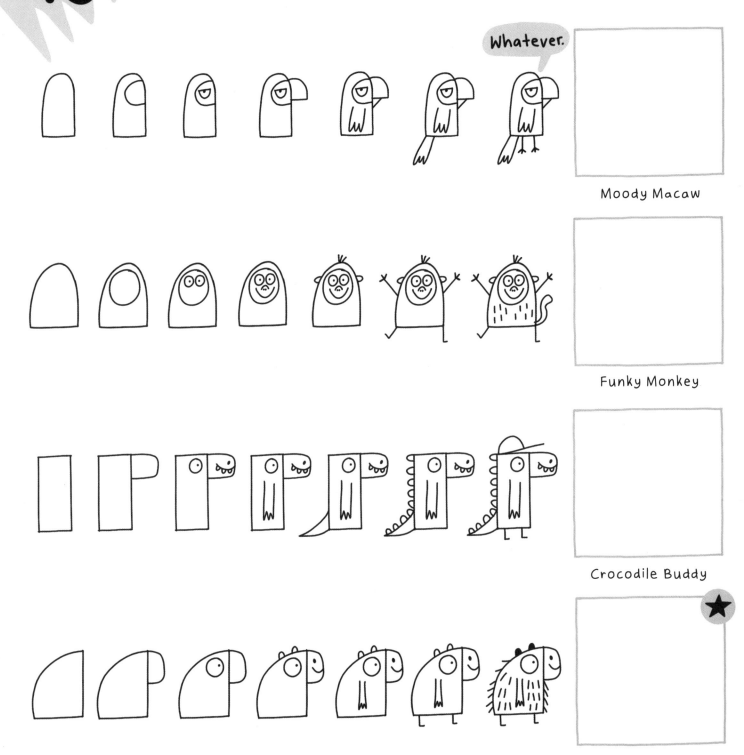

Whatever.

Moody Macaw

Funky Monkey

Crocodile Buddy

Capybara-bara

FUN FACT

The capybara is the largest rodent in the world!

Lemur on a Vine

Python 'round a Tree

Hello.

Friendly Tiger

Tapir on Skates

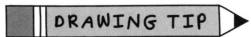 **DRAWING TIP**

You can draw a scarf like the one on Tapir
for any of these guys (but maybe not for the snake)!

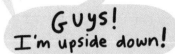

Guys!
I'm upside down!

Fuzzy Orangutan

Slothy

★

Serious Chameleon

CHOMP

Piranha Chomp-Chomp

 ★ FUN FACT

Chameleons change colors for different reasons—to cool off or warm up, to blend in or to stand out, but they can't suddenly look like your checkered tablecloth! That's a myth!

RAIN FOREST FUNTIVITY

What kind of umbrellas do these animals have?

(Example)

YAY PETS

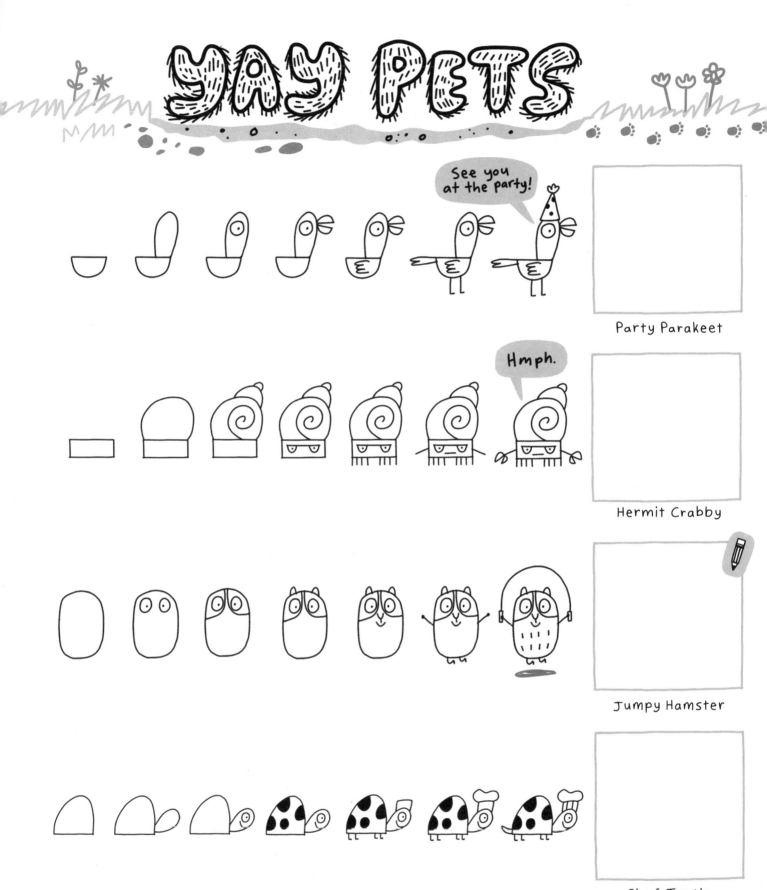

Party Parakeet

Hermit Crabby

Jumpy Hamster

Chef Turtle

DRAWING TIP

Add a little shadow under the hamster
to make it look like he's really off the ground.

Funny Bunny

Guinea Pig Pal

Blub. Blub.

Fish in a Bowl

I think you need a bath.

TIME TO IMAGINE!

What does your imaginary pet look like?

Imaginary Pet

FUN FACT

When guinea pigs do that little excited hop in the air it's known as "popcorning."

JUST CATS

 Because cats are AMAZING!

Cranky Cat

Box Cat

Sleepy Cat (Shh)

I'm so FLUFFY!

Fluffy Cat

 **FUN FACT** A bunch of cats is called a "clowder." This page is a clowder of cats.

JUST DOGS

Because birds— I mean dogs— are the BEST!

Skater Dog

Treats please.

Happy Dog

Poofy Dog

Spotty Dog

FUN FACT

Dogs hear sounds four times farther away than we can.

PET SCENE-IT

Draw some pets on the pool floats and on the beach towels.

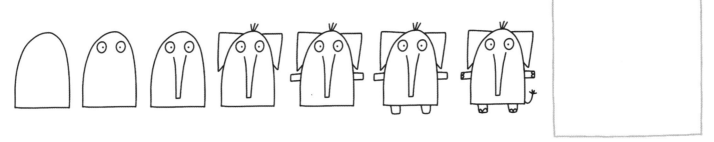

Elephant Stomp-Stomp

Z-Zebra

I have tusks!

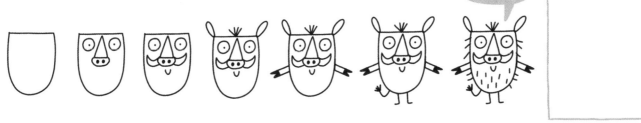

Warthog with Tusks

Cool Leopard

DRAWING TIP

You can use this leopard body to make a panther, tiger, and cheetah too.

Not Lying Lion

Just Giraffe ★

Rrrrhinoceros!

Slurpy Anteater

★ FUN FACT

Giraffe tongues are blueish-purple!

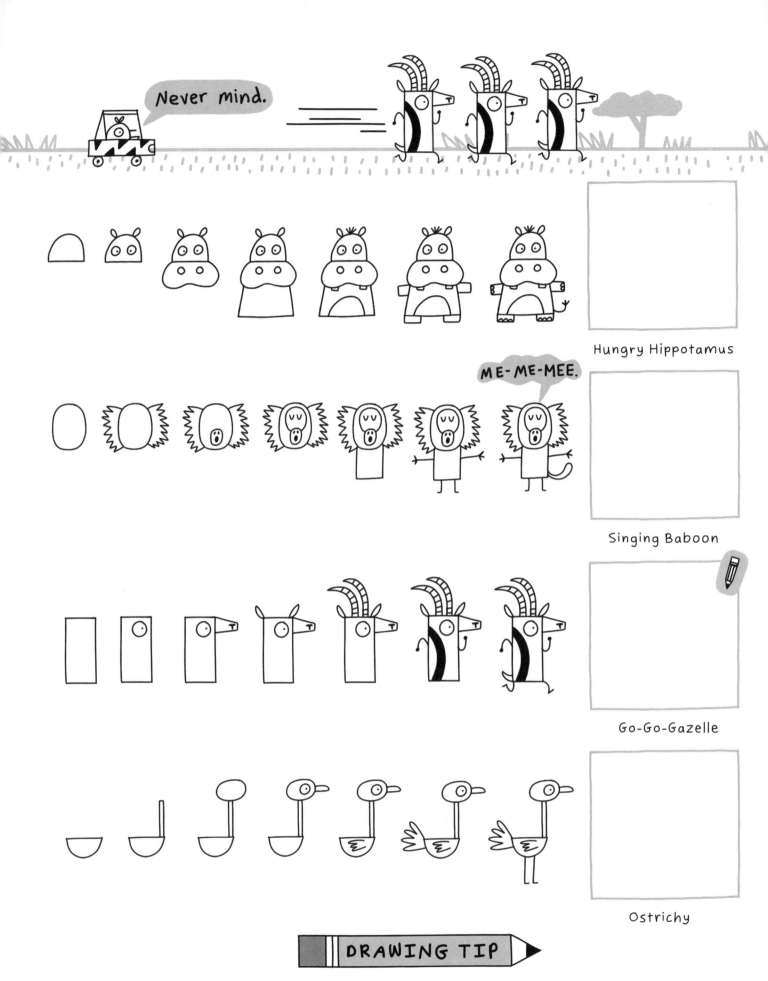

Hungry Hippotamus

Singing Baboon

Go-Go-Gazelle

Ostrichy

DRAWING TIP

To show an animal running, curve the front arm up and the other one down.
Then do the opposite with the legs. Front one curved down, back one curved up.

SAVANNA FUNTIVITY

Decorate each animal's car
so they can ride in style!

(Example)

Just Giraffes's car

Z-Zebra's electric car

Rrrrhinoceros's truck

Slurpy Anteater's jeep

Ostrichy's van

Go-Go-Gazelle's race car

SAVANNA FUNTIVITY

Facial expressions can really bring a character to life.
Here are some to practice in the space below!

HAPPY   MAD   CURIOUS   SCARED   GIDDY

SAD   TIRED   UNSURE   BORED   GROSSED OUT

Draw different expressions
to give these monkeys faces.

IN THE WOODS

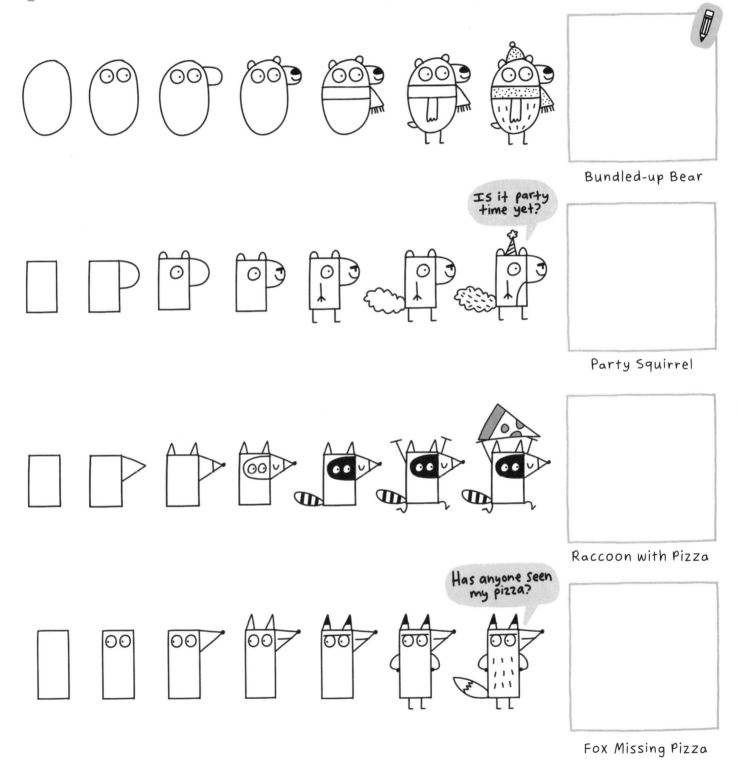

Bundled-up Bear

Party Squirrel

Is it party time yet?

Raccoon with Pizza

Has anyone seen my pizza?

Fox Missing Pizza

DRAWING TIP

Adding little dots to scarves and hats gives them a super cozy look.

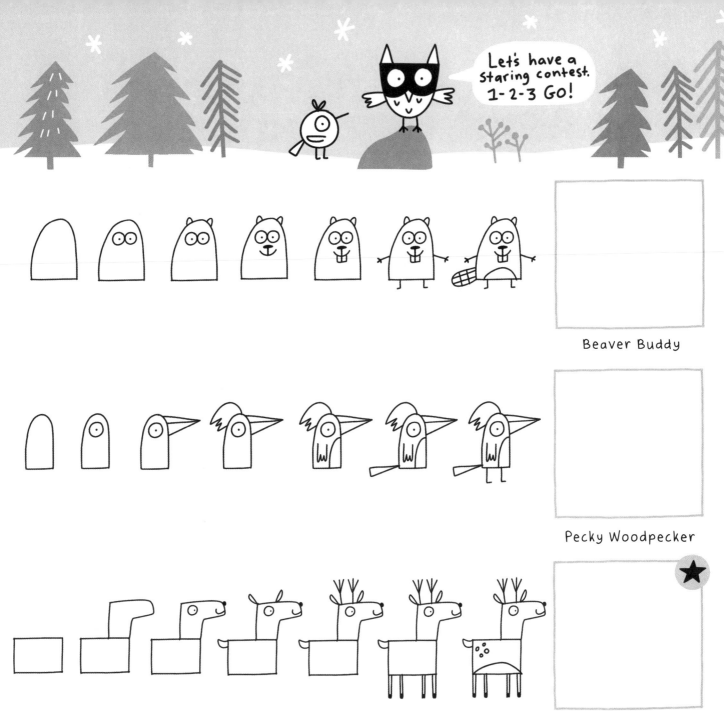

Beaver Buddy

Pecky Woodpecker

Deary Deer

Skunky

toot

FUN FACT

Deer can jump up to ten feet high.
That's as tall as a basketball hoop!

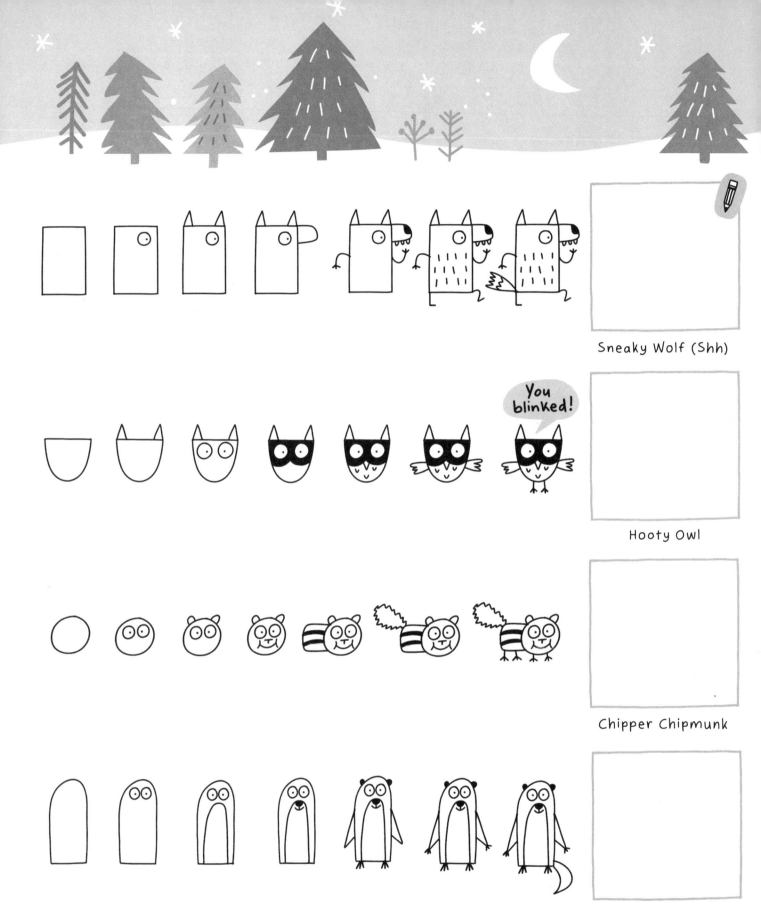

Sneaky Wolf (Shh)

You blinked!

Hooty Owl

Chipper Chipmunk

Otterly Adorable

 DRAWING TIP

Little lines are a fun and easy way to draw fur.

CAN'T REST.
MUST DRAW.

Little Badger Friend

Mooooose

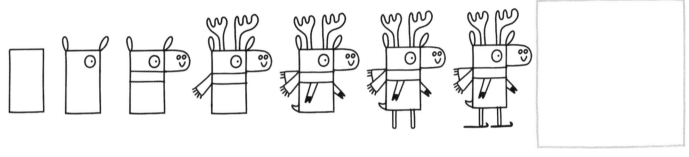

Who wants
a hug?

Cuddly Porcupine

Bat-Bat

FUN FACT

What do badgers, lions, bears, and sharks have in common?
Their babies are all called cubs!

WOODS FUNTIVITY

You can take almost any shape and make it into a cute bird. Here are some examples to practice. But feel free to make up your own with your genius imagination.

OCEAN DIVE

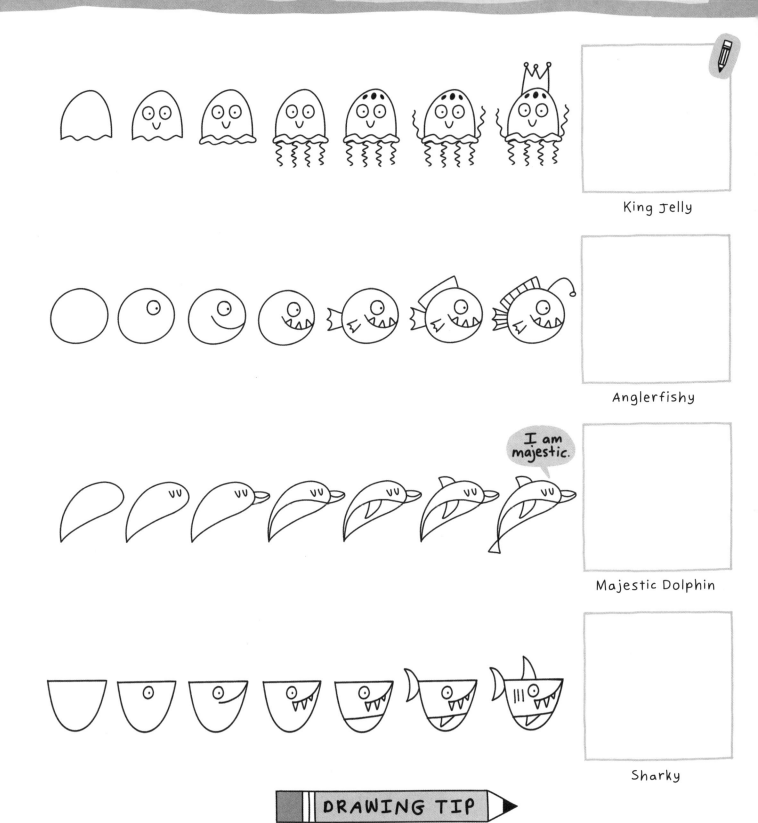

King Jelly

Anglerfishy

I am majestic.

Majestic Dolphin

Sharky

DRAWING TIP

Jellyfish can have up to 15 tentacles but you don't need to draw them all. Keep it simple and just draw a few!

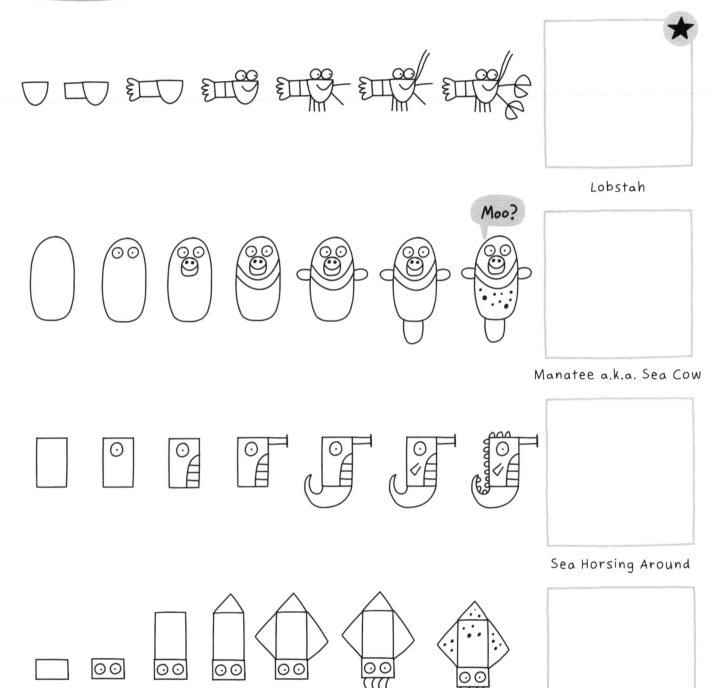

Lobstah

Manatee a.k.a. Sea Cow

Sea Horsing Around

Squidy-Squid

FUN FACT

Lobsters have tiny hairs on their legs
that allow them to taste food.

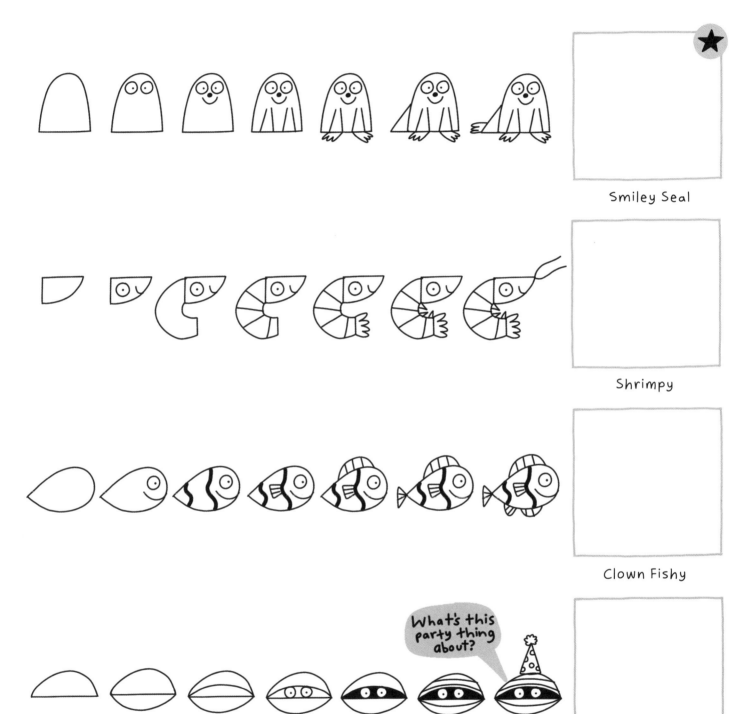

Smiley Seal

Shrimpy

Clown Fishy

What's this party thing about?

Keep Calm & Clam On

FUN FACT

Seals can sleep underwater!

OCEAN SCENE-IT

Did someone order a pizza?
Draw your favorite ocean animals in the scene below!

super cute Babies

Mini Monkey Baby

★

Spiky Crocodile Baby

What a cutie!

Baby Cat

Tiny Tiger Baby

★

FUN FACT

Crocodile babies hatch out of eggs buried in the sand. Their mothers carry them to the water in their mouths, keeping their jaws open!

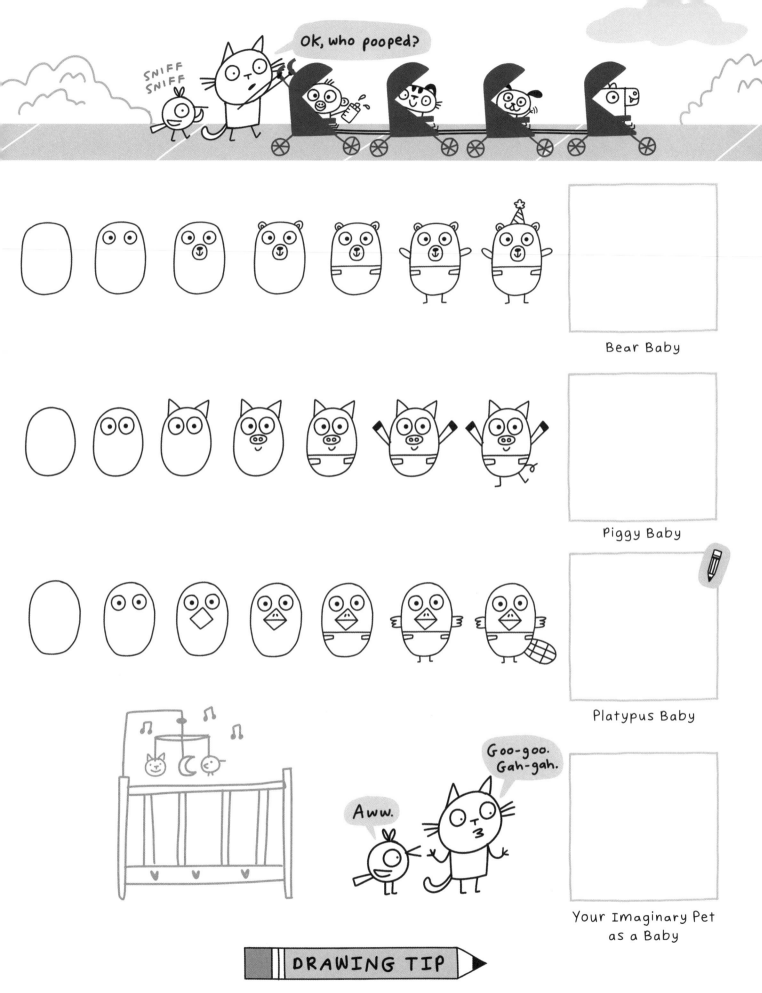

Bear Baby

Piggy Baby

Platypus Baby

Your Imaginary Pet
as a Baby

DRAWING TIP

A diamond shape is perfect for drawing bills and beaks that face forward.

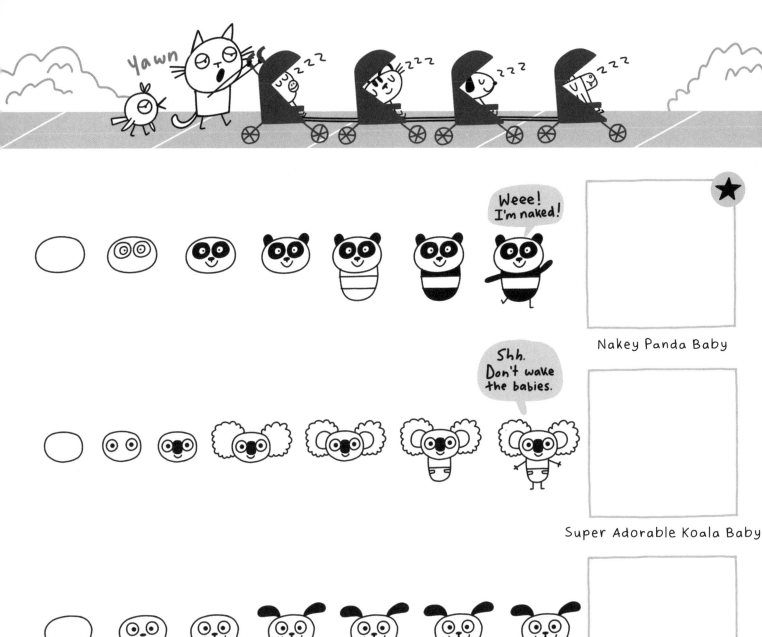

Nakey Panda Baby

Super Adorable Koala Baby

Puppy Baby

Chicky Baby

★ FUN FACT

Panda babies are tiny when they are born and only weigh around 100 grams—that's about as heavy as a stick of butter!

babies FUNTIVITY

Drawing animal babies is easy once you know the secret trick. Ready?
All you have to do is draw their head and give them a teeny-tiny body.
Then it's a **CUTENESS OVERLOAD**! P.S. Big eyes help too!

Follow the example below to create your own versions of animal babies.

(Example)

Rabbit Baby

Mouse Baby

Fox Baby

Goat Baby

Raccoon Baby

Octopus Baby

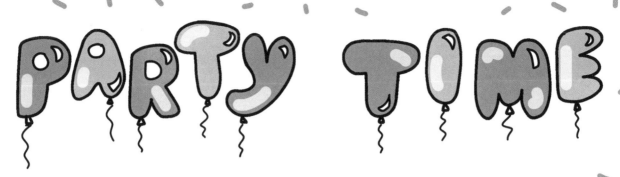

PARTY TIME

These animals are off to a party!
Let's make them look their best.

Draw them some nifty accessories from the wardrobe.

READY TO PARTAY!

Wow! I look amazing!

I'm a trendsetter.

PARTY FUNTIVITY

What is Slurpy Anteater saying about Party Squirrel's balloon? What does Party Squirrel's balloon look like?

Draw your own party animal comic below!

Tiger Baby is getting her picture taken at the party photo booth. What kind of faces does she make?

(Psst. If you need inspiration, flip back to page 24.)

PARTY SCENE-IT

It's almost the end of the book! Time to celebrate your hard work.

Finish decorating and get the snacks ready. Draw in your party animals and let's DANCE!

You also get a NEW CAR!!!

WINNER

WINNER

Just kidding. But you DO get an official **FUN ANIMALS** club card.

Draw a picture of yourself in the square and **CONQUER THE WORLD!**

Or ya know...just keep drawing!